Travel Through
Japan

Joe Fullman

QED Publishing

First published in the UK in 2007 by
QED Publishing
A Quarto Group company
226 City Road
London EC1V 2TT

www.qed-publishing.co.uk

A catalogue record for this book is available from the British Library.

ISBN 978 1 84538 757 0

Written by Joe Fullman
Designed by Chhaya Sajwan (Q2A Media)
Editor Honor Head
Picture Researcher Sujatha Menon (Q2A Media)

Publisher Steve Evans
Creative Director Zeta Davies
Senior Editor Hannah Ray

Printed and bound in China

Picture credits

Key: t = top, b = bottom, c = centre,
l = left, r = right, FC = front cover

Words in **bold** can be found in the glossary on page 31.

Contents

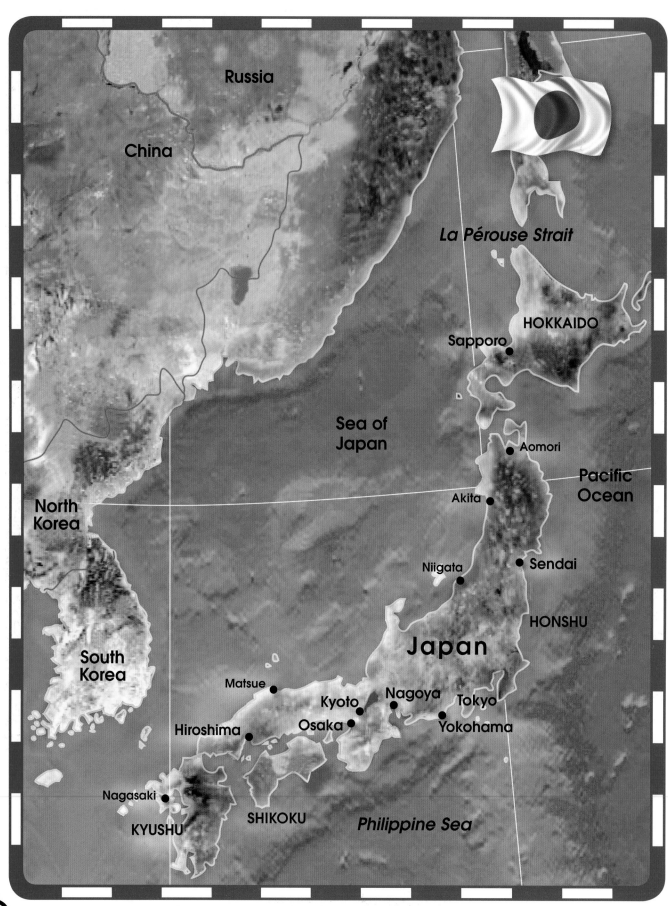

Russia

China

La Pérouse Strait

HOKKAIDO

Sapporo

Sea of
Japan

Aomori

Pacific
Ocean

North
Korea

Akita

Niigata

Sendai

HONSHU

South
Korea

Japan

Matsue

Kyoto

Nagoya

Tokyo

Osaka

Hiroshima

Yokohama

Nagasaki

KYUSHU

SHIKOKU

Philippine Sea

Where in the world is Japan?

Japan is made up of a group of islands off the eastern coast of **Asia**. It is a very mountainous country, entirely surrounded by water. To the north is the La Pérouse Strait, the Sea of Japan is to the west, to the south is the Philippine Sea, and to the east is the Pacific Ocean. Its nearest neighbouring countries are Russia, which lies across the sea to the north and north-west, and North Korea, South Korea and China, which lie across the sea to the west. Taiwan lies to the south-west.

Japan is the world's 62nd-largest country, but has the world's tenth-largest population with over 120 million people. Most of these people live in Japan's many cities.

Did you know?

OFFICIAL NAME: Japan

LOCATION: Eastern Asia

SURROUNDING COUNTRIES: Russia, North Korea, South Korea, China and Taiwan

SURROUNDING SEAS AND OCEANS: La Pérouse Strait, Sea of Japan, East China Sea, Philippine Sea, Pacific Ocean

LENGTH OF COASTLINE: 29 751km

CAPITAL: Tokyo

AREA: 374 744sq km

POPULATION: 127 417 200

LIFE EXPECTANCY: Male: 76 years Female: 83 years

RELIGIONS: Shintoism, Buddhism, Christianity

LANGUAGES: Japanese

CLIMATE: Cool in the north, **temperate** in the centre, **tropical** in the south. There's a **typhoon** season in September.

HIGHEST MOUNTAIN: Mount Fuji (3776m high)

MAJOR RIVERS: Shinano (367km long), Tone (322km long)

CURRENCY: Yen

What is Japan like?

Japan is made up of many islands. There are over 3900 of them in total. However, most of these islands are very small and do not have people living on them. Nearly all of the people in Japan live on just four main islands, which are called Hokkaido, Shikoku, Kyushu and Honshu. Honshu is the largest island. Over 80 per cent of the Japanese population lives here. This is where you'll find the country's largest cities, including Kyoto and the capital, Tokyo.

Mountains and plains

As you travel around Japan, you'll see many mountains. Over three-quarters of Japan's land is made up of mountain **ranges.** Everywhere you look, great towering peaks rise up into the sky. Most of the country's villages and cities have been built on flat **plains** between the mountains. Because there is so little flat land in Japan, Japanese homes are often very small and are built close to one another. Japanese cities are filled with **skyscrapers** which don't take up much ground space.

Many Japanese villages are surrounded by tall, snow-capped mountains and thick pine forests.

Tokyo is Japan's largest and richest city. Its centre is filled with towering skyscrapers.

Earthquakes and volcanoes

If you were to spend some time in Japan, you might feel the earth shake. This is an earthquake, a common occurrence in Japan. Most earthquakes are small and harmless. Every now and then, however, Japan is shaken by a large earthquake which may topple buildings and cause giant cracks to appear in the roads.
As you travel around, you may also see volcanoes oozing red-hot lava. Japan has many active volcanoes.

The latest gadgets

Most Japanese people live in cities. As you walk along the streets, you'll see shops selling lots of electronic gadgets, such as mobile phones, MP3 players and computer-game consoles. Japan is famous for its electronic products, which it sells throughout the world. In Japan, trends, fashions and technology change fast.

Japan's factories produce many electronic toys, such as this robot dog.

Different climates

Japan is a very long country, stretching for over 3000km from north to south. If you travelled from northern Japan to southern Japan, you would pass through a number of different climates. Hokkaido, the most northerly island, has very cold, snowy winters and cool summers. Honshu, Japan's largest island, has a milder climate. Further south, the island of Kyushu enjoys mild winters and hot, humid summers.

Much of Japan enjoys hot summers when fields of colourful flowers, such as these marigolds, come into bloom.

Cold winters, wet summers

If you spent the winter in Japan, you'd probably prefer to stay on the eastern side of the country. The winters here tend to be clear, dry and mild. Winters on the western side of the country are much more fierce. The people who live here have to wrap up warm to protect themselves against bitterly cold winds blowing in from Russia and heavy snows. Japan's summers can be very wet, with many rainy days. In late summer, Japan is often hit by revolving tropical storms known as typhoons. Typhoon winds can blow at up to 200km per hour (that's over one and half times quicker than cars can travel on the motorway!) and can cause a lot of damage to buildings.

During the annual Sapporo Snow and Ice Festival on the island of Hokkaido, people carve giant statues out of ice.

During the rainy season in the summer, downpours are common and people carry umbrellas to keep dry.

YOU'VE GOT MAIL

Yokohama, where I live, is a port on the east coast of Honshu. In June, it rains almost every day. You have to wear plastic shoes and a raincoat to keep dry when you go out. When it has been raining a lot, the streets are filled with puddles, which are fun to splash around in. Sometimes the winds are very strong. Then it can be difficult to walk and you have to stay indoors. When you look out of the window, you can see people's umbrellas being blown inside out by the wind.
Keiko

Up mountains and along rivers

The green-blue waters of Lake Okama fill the crater of Mount Zao, an **extinct** volcano on the island of Honshu.

Great ranges of snow-capped peaks run down the centre of Japan. There are 15 mountains that stand over 3000m high. Many of these are **dormant** volcanoes. This includes Japan's highest mountain, Mount Fuji, which stands at 3776m. Most of Japan's mountains are covered in thick pine forest.

Bridges and tunnels

As you travel around Japan, you will notice many bridges and tunnels. The country's villages and cities are often cut off from each other by mountains. Over the centuries, the Japanese people have built tunnels through the mountains and bridges over **gorges** to link the communities.

The top of Mount Fuji, Japan's highest mountain, is covered in a thick layer of snow.

Short rivers

Most of Japan's rivers begin in the central mountains and run down into either the Pacific Ocean in the East or the Sea of Japan in the West. Because Japan is very narrow, its rivers are not very long. (The longest, the Shinano, is 367km.) They are, however, steep and fast-flowing. After heavy rains, there is often flooding.

Shrinking lakes

Japan also has many lakes, some of which have formed in the craters of extinct volcanoes, such as Lake Towada on Honshu Island. The country's largest lake is Lake Biwa, also in Honshu. It is not as large as it used to be because the nearby cities of Kyoto and Osaka have used a lot of its water for drinking and industry.

These Japanese macaques keep warm in winter by bathing in a natural hot pool near a volcano.

Over 60 per cent of Japan is covered in forest. Many animals live here, including giant flying squirrels, macaques (a type of monkey) and wild boar.

Earthquakes, floods and volcanoes

Japanese people have to take care to avoid a number of natural hazards that affect their country. These natural events can cause a lot of damage, but the Japanese have learned to live with these dangers.

Earthquakes

Japan lies on a part of the Earth's surface where earthquakes are common. Every year there are hundreds of minor earthquakes. Most of these can barely be felt. However, every ten years or so Japan suffers a massive earthquake. The people take many precautions against earthquake damage. Their buildings are built so that in an earthquake they will sway rather than fall down. As soon as an earthquake begins, electricity and gas supplies are cut off to prevent fire, and trains are automatically stopped from running. All Japanese schoolchildren learn earthquake emergency training.

A large earthquake can cause a lot of damage, blocking the streets with fallen rubble.

Volcanoes

Japan has over 60 active volcanoes. Many of these regularly send eruptions of red-hot lava spewing out onto the surrounding land. Though spectacular, Japan's volcanoes rarely cause much damage to property. The Japanese have learned to build their towns well out of the way of most eruptions.

Floods and landslides

Japan's most common natural hazards are caused by water. At the end of winter, melting snow in the mountains pours into rivers which then burst their banks and flood towns and cities. In summer, heavy rains can cause landslides. This happens when soil on the side of a hill becomes waterlogged and heavy. Eventually it gets so heavy that it slides down the hill causing a great deal of damage.

After a big storm, floodwater can quickly fill a city street, stopping cars in their tracks.

These children are practising their earthquake drill. They have put on their protective hoods and are under their desks.

Once a month at school we practise our earthquake drill. We're taught to get under our desks and hold on to its legs. We then put on hoods which help to protect us from falling rubble, flying glass and heat, and file out of the classroom to the playground. Here the teacher takes a register. We stand in the centre of the playground away from the school buildings, which might fall down if there is a real earthquake.
Cato

At school

In Japan, children start school at the age of six. They attend Elementary School for six years, and then go on to Middle School for three years. These nine years of schooling are **compulsory**. After this, the children have the choice to go on to High School for another three years. Finally, if their grades are good enough, they can go to University for four years.

Baseball is very popular in Japan. Many schools have baseball clubs where children can practise their skills after their normal lessons.

The fifth of May is Children's Day in Japan, a national holiday to celebrate children.

Many Japanese children have to wear a uniform when they go to school.

Subjects

Japanese children are taught a wide range of subjects. At Elementary School, students learn Japanese, maths, science, history, geography, music, physical education, food technology and information technology. Some students learn English, although this is usually only taught to older children. Students are also taught the traditional Japanese art of shodo – which is writing Japanese symbols using a brush and ink.

Activities

Outside of their official classes, children can also take part in a range of other school activities. They can play sports, such as baseball and football, or learn traditional Japanese crafts such as origami (paper folding) and ikebana (flower arranging). They are also taken on school trips to historical sites.

In the morning we had maths and Japanese lessons. We then ate our lunch together in the classroom. The class is divided into a number of small groups. Each day, one group takes its turn to serve the others their food. In the afternoon we had my favourite lesson – physical education. Then we played baseball. Finally, we cleaned up the classroom together. We do this every day before going home.
Takumi

On a school trip, Japanese children will often wear brightly coloured caps, so that they can be easily seen by motorists – and their teacher!

Crowded cities

Because there is so little flat land in Japan, the cities are filled with tall buildings, which take up less space on the ground.

Visit any Japanese city and there's one thing you're sure to see – people. Japan has the tenth-largest population in the world, with over 120 million people. Around 80 per cent of them live in cities. Japan has 12 cities with a population of over a million. Most of these are located on the east side of the country.

Close together

Japan has a very high **population density**. In other words, it is very crowded. There is only a small amount of space for people to live because of the mountains. On average, there are over 340 people living in each square kilometre. In America, there are just 29 people per square kilometre.

Capital city

Tokyo is the capital of Japan and the country's largest city. It is also where many of Japan's most important businesses and government buildings are located. Over 12 million people live in the city centre and over 30 million in the Greater Tokyo Area – that's a quarter of Japan's population.

People fill the streets of Shibuya, one of Tokyo's most crowded districts, where there is a population density of over 12 000 people per sq km.

My name is Kenta. I live in an apartment in Tokyo where I share a room with my brother, Naoki. At home, I like to play computer games and watch cartoons, called **Anime**, on TV. Sometimes, I read **Manga** comic books. When I'm out with my friends, I also like to play a traditional Japanese game called bei-goma. To play, everyone must spin a top at the same time. The person who gets their top to spin for the longest time wins the game.

These children are reading Manga stories, a type of comic book popular in Japan.

Wooden houses

At the centre of most Japanese cities, buildings tend to be made of steel and concrete. However, in the suburbs where the majority of the people live, houses are often built out of wood. Many Japanese houses have floors made of tatami (straw mats), which keep the rooms cool in summer and warm in winter. It is polite to remove your shoes when entering a Japanese home.

Japanese families traditionally sit on the floor around a low table to eat their meals.

Farming regions

As you travel around Japan, you'll see many farms, but not as many as you would have done in the past. Forty years ago, one in three people in Japan worked on a farm. Since then, Japan's **industries** have become very succesful and many people have changed jobs to work in them. Today, only around one in 20 people still work on farms. Nearly all Japanese farms are situated on the country's flat plains.

Growing rice

The most important crop grown in Japan is rice, as it is the main part of the Japanese diet. Most of Japan's rice is grown on the main island of Honshu, on the Kanto Plain, the country's largest area of flat land. Rice is grown in flooded fields known as paddy fields. Japan's high rainfall helps the crop to grow well. Despite the country's small amount of farmland, Japan grows over 95 per cent of the rice it eats.

These farmers are using modern farming equipment to plant rice in the huge paddy fields.

This girl is feeding hay to cows on a dairy farm.

Though Japan has many modern farms, some people still use traditional methods, picking their crops by hand and wearing straw hats for protection against the Sun.

My name is Misaki. My family has a small farm on the island of Shikoku where we grow a number of crops including rice, barley, tomatoes and onions. My mother and father look after the farm during the week, but my brother and I help at weekends. Every week my father travels to the main island of Honshu to sell our vegetables at one of the big markets there. The farm doesn't make a lot of money, so we get a **grant** from the government to help us pay our bills.

Cattle and crops

There is very little good **pasture** in Japan. Most of the country's cattle are reared on the northern island of Hokkaido. The farms here supply much of the country's butter, milk and beef. Barley is also grown here. To the south, on the hot, humid island of Kyushu, tropical fruits, such as mandarins and pineapples, are grown. There are also a number of tea plantations here. Throughout the country, Japan's forests are **logged** to supply timber for fuel, paper and building materials.

Getting around

Japan's four main islands were once separated by stretches of sea, and people could only travel between them by boat or plane. However, in the past fifty years they have been linked together by a number of bridges and tunnels. Some of these are very long. The 54km Seikan Tunnel between Hokkaido and Honshu is the longest railway tunnel in the world. It is also the deepest, running 240m below the surface of the sea. The Akashi-Kaikyo Bridge between Honshu and Awaji Island is the world's longest **suspension bridge**, measuring 1991m.

Before the Akashi-Kaikyo bridge was built in 1998, people had to use a ferry to cross this water.

Today I got the bullet train for the first time from Tokyo to Fukushima, where my auntie and uncle live. I was a bit scared at first because I know the train travels very quickly and I thought I might feel ill. However, the train ride was very smooth. My mum also made me feel better by telling me these trains are very safe. I remember my pen pal telling me in a letter that trains in his country were often late. Sometimes they were even cancelled. This never happens in Japan. No bullet train is more than a few seconds late.
Haru

Bullet trains

Japan's most famous forms of transport are its shinkansen, or bullet trains. These trains travel around the country at great speeds of up to 240km per hour. Long distances can be covered very quickly. The bullet train network was introduced in 1964. Since then, the trains have carried over three billion passengers.

Space to land

Japan's road and rail links are so good that few people use planes to travel around the country. However, Japan does have many visitors from other countries who travel in by plane. This used to be a problem as planes need a lot of flat space on which to take off and land. Mountain-filled Japan does not have much flat space. To solve this, the Kansai International Airport in Osaka Bay was built off the coast, on an artificial island in the middle of the sea. It is linked to the mainland by a bridge.

Kansai International Airport sits on a specially built, square-shaped island just off the coast of mainland Japan.

Food and drink

As you travel around Japan, you will be offered many different types of food. Wherever you go, however, you will be served rice. Rice is the main food of Japan and is eaten at most meals. In fact the word for meal in Japan is 'gohan', which also means rice. Because people in Japan use **chopsticks** to eat their food, their rice is usually cooked so that the grains stick together which makes it easier to pick up.

Japan has many fish markets where people can come and buy the latest fresh catches.

My name is Tomoko. I live in Sapporo. At home, my favourite food is sukiyaki. This is a mixture of vegetables and meat cooked with a **soy sauce** and served with raw egg dip. When I'm out, I also like to try different foreign foods, such as hamburgers.

Lots of fish

The Japanese have more fishing boats and eat more fish than any other country on Earth. Fishing takes place all around the country's long coastline, as well as out at sea. Fish are also farmed in the country's inland sea, the area of water which separates three of Japan's four main islands, Honshu, Shikoku and Kyushu.

Popular foods and drinks

There are a number of delicious foods which are common all over Japan. Miso is a mixture of soya beans and barley, and is often used to flavour soup. Sushi is another of the country's most famous foods – it is small pieces of cold rice, usually served with slices of raw fish, shellfish and seaweed. Tempura is the name given to shellfish and vegetables that have been fried in a light, crisp batter. Green tea, served without milk or sugar, is one of Japan's most popular drinks.

In some sushi bars, customers can choose their dishes from a revolving conveyor belt.

A changing diet

The Japanese diet has changed a lot in the last 50 years. More meat, bread and dairy products are now eaten. Many cities also have branches of Western fast-food chains which are very popular, particularly with young people. However, most Japanese people still eat very healthily. Japan has the highest **life expectancy** in the world thanks to the healthy food that most Japanese people eat.

Traditional Japanese teacups do not have handles.

Japanese tea sets always have either three or six cups, never four. Four is an unlucky number in Japan.

Religion

Shintoism and Buddhism are the two main religions in Japan. Many Japanese people follow both these religions.

Shintoism

Shinto is Japan's oldest religion. Shinto followers believe that everything in the natural world – every tree, every rock, every plant – has its own god. There are thousands of Shinto gods. It is common for Japanese people to have Shinto **shrines** in their homes where they say prayers. Shinto has no holy writings, no leaders and no forms of group worship.

Buddhism

Buddhism was first developed in India and China, and later brought to Japan. There is no god in Buddhism. Buddhist teaching is about achieving peace through meditation, or deep thought. Buddhists believe in **reincarnation**. The city of Kyoto has over 1600 Buddhist temples.

Kinkakuji, or the 'Golden Pavilion', is an important Buddhist shrine. Built in 1397, it was rebuilt in 1955 following a fire.

Sport

In Japan, people enjoy traditional Japanese activities, such as sumo and judo, as well as modern international sports, including baseball and football.

Sumo wrestling

Sumo is a very exciting and popular type of Japanese wrestling. Sumo wrestlers face each other in a ring marked with a rope. To win, one wrestler must push the other out of the ring, or trip them over onto the ground. Sumo wrestlers are very big. The biggest weigh over 180kg. Wrestlers wear coloured loincloths called 'fundoshi'. Top sumo wrestlers are big celebrities in Japan.

Sumo wrestlers stamp on the ground before each bout to try and put off their opponents.

Judo

Like sumo, judo is a type of wrestling. The wrestlers try to throw each other onto the ground using different holds and moves. Judo is one of the sports performed at the Olympics. Judo wrestlers are much smaller than sumo wrestlers! They usually wear a white, loose-fitting top and trousers.

Judo wrestlers wear a white uniform known as a judogi.

Kendo

Kendo is a type of sword fighting using wooden swords made from bamboo. Competitors wear masks and chest guards to protect themselves from getting hurt. To win, one opponent must strike the other on the head or chest with their sword.

Industry and technology

Japan has the second-largest **economy** in the world, after the USA. If you were to walk through the centre of a big Japanese city, such as Tokyo or Sapporo, you would see shops selling lots of different Japanese products. Japan also sells its goods to other countries. Many of its biggest companies are known throughout the world. Most Japanese industries are in the big cities on the Pacific side of the country.

Hi-tech goods

Japan is perhaps most famous for its hi-tech goods – TVs, DVD players, digital cameras and computer-game consoles, which are sold around the world. You probably have some Japanese goods in your house. See if you can find out what they are.

Nuclear power

Japan does not have many natural fuel reserves, such as supplies of coal or gas. Instead, it has to **import** these from abroad. Over 80 per cent of Japan's electricity is made using fuels that have been bought from other countries. The other 20 per cent is produced by 55 **nuclear power stations** that are spread around the country.

Nuclear power stations contain many harmful substances, which must be protected behind huge walls of thick concrete.

More and more people in Japan are training to become chefs.

Japan's cars are among the most advanced in the world.

Japanese workers

Fifty years ago, most people in Japan worked on farms or had jobs in heavy industries, such as iron and steel production. Today, the majority of Japanese people have jobs in the **service industries**, working in restaurants, shops, banks and in leisure and tourism.

Activity ideas

1 Japan is made up of a group of islands known as an archipelago. Carry out an Internet search to find out about different archipelagos around the world, such as the British Isles. Do they have as many islands as Japan? How many of these islands have people living on them?

2 Use an atlas of the world to find other places on the same **latitude** as Tokyo, Japan. Using the Internet, find out if these other countries have the same amount of rainfall or the same average temperature as Japan, or if they differ. Plot the results on a chart to compare weather conditions in these countries.

3 Plan an imaginary trip around Japan. If you could visit just six places in Japan, where would you go? Why? How would you get to Japan? How long would it take you? How would you get to the different places in Japan?

4 Make a 3D map of Japan using paper-mâché. Look at the map of Japan on page 4 of this book and use it to copy the rough shape of the four main islands of Japan onto a sheet of card. Crumple up pieces of paper and stick them over the shapes to build up the 'land'. Remember to make lots of peaks, as Japan has many mountains. Glue these firmly in place. Coat in PVA glue, and cover the whole model carefully with a sheet of tissue paper. Push the paper carefully into all the inlets and coves you have created. Repeat this step until you have a smooth surface and leave it to dry. Then paint and label your model.

5 Research and write a project on Japanese samurai warriors. Who were they? When did they live? How did they protect themselves?

6 Using the Internet, find out about the sort of clothes people wear in Japan. What was the Japanese style of dress in olden times? How do modern Japanese people dress? Draw and label a picture of someone wearing traditional Japanese clothes. Why do you think they wore clothes like this?

7 Search through cookery books and on the Internet to find a recipe for some Japanese foods, such as sushi or sukiyaki. With an adult, cook the foods together, and create a pretend restaurant area where you can create menus and take turns to act as a waiter and diner, before eating the food. You could also buy some examples of different Japanese foods and taste them, and perhaps write reviews of the food. How do they compare to British foods? You could make a display of the reports of the food.

NOTE FOR ADULTS:
Please ensure that children do not suffer from any food allergies before making or eating any food.

8 Using the Internet and some travel brochures, find the images and pictures of Japan most often shown to tourists travelling to the country. Print out the pictures to make a collage of 'Tourist Japan'. What are the most popular places in Japan? What ideas and images do travel websites use to sell Japan as a travel destination? Create a poster, encouraging people to visit Japan.

9 Look on the Internet and in your local library for books and information on origami – the Japanese art of folding pieces of paper into different shapes, such as animals, dinosaurs, flowers and boats. Cut some paper into squares and try some origami for yourself.

10 Make a fact file about the Seikan Rail Tunnel between Hokkaido and Honshu, the longest and deepest railway tunnel in the world. Afterwards, you could make a working model. (You'll need a model train for this activity.) Make the tunnel by bending a sheet of thin card and attaching it to a base – the side from a strong cardboard box will do, or a large piece of corrugated cardboard. Paint the model with brown paint mixed with a little PVA glue for strength. Tear strips of blue tissue, crepe and cellophane in shades of blue, and stick them to the base board beside the tunnel on either side – this will be the sea. You could even add clay sea creatures. When everything is dry, send your model train through the tunnel!

11 Imagine you are travelling across Japan, using its super-fast bullet trains to pass over bridges and through tunnels. Alternatively, imagine you are also climbing one of the country's many high mountains. Write entries in an imaginary blog about your journey. What do you see? Who do you meet? Does anything funny happen to you? What do you discover about Japan?

13 See if your local library has any children's Manga comic books. Make up a story and write it in a Manga-style comic strip using coloured pens and pencils.

12 Write a tourist leaflet describing a city in Japan. What does the city look like? What sort of buildings does it have? Remember to use language that will make people want to visit.

14 Carry out research on the Internet and in the library, and then write a report about sumo wrestling. What are the rules of the sport? How does one sumo wrestler beat another? What do sumo wrestlers wear? What do sumo wrestlers eat? How often are sumo competitions held?

Glossary

Anime Cartoon programmes shown on TV.

Asia One of the seven continents that make up all the Earth's land. The others are North America, South America, Europe, Africa, Australia and Antarctica.

chopsticks Two thin pieces of wood used to eat food.

compulsory Something that has to be done.

dormant Inactive or asleep.

economy Everything to do with the making, selling and buying of goods.

extinct Something which is no longer alive or active. A volcano that has stopped erupting is extinct.

gorges Deep valleys with steep sides.

grant A gift or loan of money.

import Buying goods from other countries.

industries Companies that make products.

latitude Distance from the equator (an imaginary circle around the middle of the earth, shown on most maps).

life expectancy The average number of years a person is expected to live – which is influenced by their lifestyle.

logged When many trees have been cut down. Logging is the cutting down of trees in order to sell them.

Manga Japanese comic books.

nuclear power stations Places that make electricity using nuclear power.

pasture Fields where farm animals, such as cows and sheep, live and eat.

plains Large areas of flat land.

population density The number of people living in a certain amount of land. If there are a lot of people, the place has a high population density.

ranges Several groups of mountains.

reincarnation Being born again in another form after death.

service industries Industries that provides services for other people, such as an entertainment show or a meal in a restaurant, rather than goods, such as cars or TVs.

shrines Small temples to a god or gods.

skyscrapers Very tall buildings.

soy sauce A dark brown sauce made from soy beans, which is popular in Japan.

suspension bridge A bridge where the weight is supported by cables hung from high towers.

temperate Mild weather where it is neither too hot nor too cold.

tropical Hot and humid, the climate of the Tropics – the areas either side of the Equator.

typhoon A severe storm with strong winds that blow in a circular movement.

Index